I0819508

THE STORY OF EVERYTHING

THE STORY OF YOU!

BY KARA NEWHOUSE ILLUSTRATED BY KATE COSGROVE

HOLIDAY HOUSE NEW YORK

This is the story of everything.

BANG!

BANG!

BANG!

Long before you came to be . . . the universe was born.

Then came the sun . . .

. . . and the planets too.

SULFUR
CONTINENTS

Long before you grew cell by cell . . .
continents formed,
sulfur steamed,
bacteria multiplied,
life evolved on Earth.

Long before you drew your first breath . . .

glug

glug

glug

. . . fish swam the seas.

Long before you took your first steps . . .

. . . amphibians crawled and hopped to land.

Long before you spoke your first word . . .

bees buzzed,

dinosaurs roared,

mammals roamed,

and a giant asteroid hurtled toward Earth.

BOOM!

Long before you played in the dirt . . .
soot filled the air,

dinosaurs disappeared,

tsunamis and wildfires raged.

And darkness fell.

Ca-caw!

Long before you laughed and sang . . .

life renewed.

Eee! Eee!

Long before you climbed and jumped . . .

primates swung from branch to branch.

Then not quite so long ago . . .

clang, beep, yippee!

. . . humans began to build, create, and play.

And on one special day . . .

lub dub, lub dub

. . . you came to be.

This is the story of everything.

This is the story of you.

Our universe is very old. It formed about 14 billion years ago. By comparison, planet Earth seems young. But it's still much older than you!

Earth formed about 4.5 billion years ago. To learn about all the things that have happened since then, scientists look at rock layers and other clues. Old rocks are at the bottom, with new rocks layered on top. Sometimes, pieces or impressions of ancient life, called fossils, can be seen in the rocks, too. Scientists who study rock layers and fossils are called geologists.

Geologists created the Geologic Time Scale as a way to learn about different parts of Earth's history. The scale shows the major changes that occurred on Earth's surface across billions of years. It also charts how life developed—from the earliest bacteria to you.

A note on sounds: We do not know exactly what sounds prehistoric creatures made. The sounds in this book were chosen based on scientists' best guesses about what was happening on Earth's surface and among living things millions and billions of years ago.

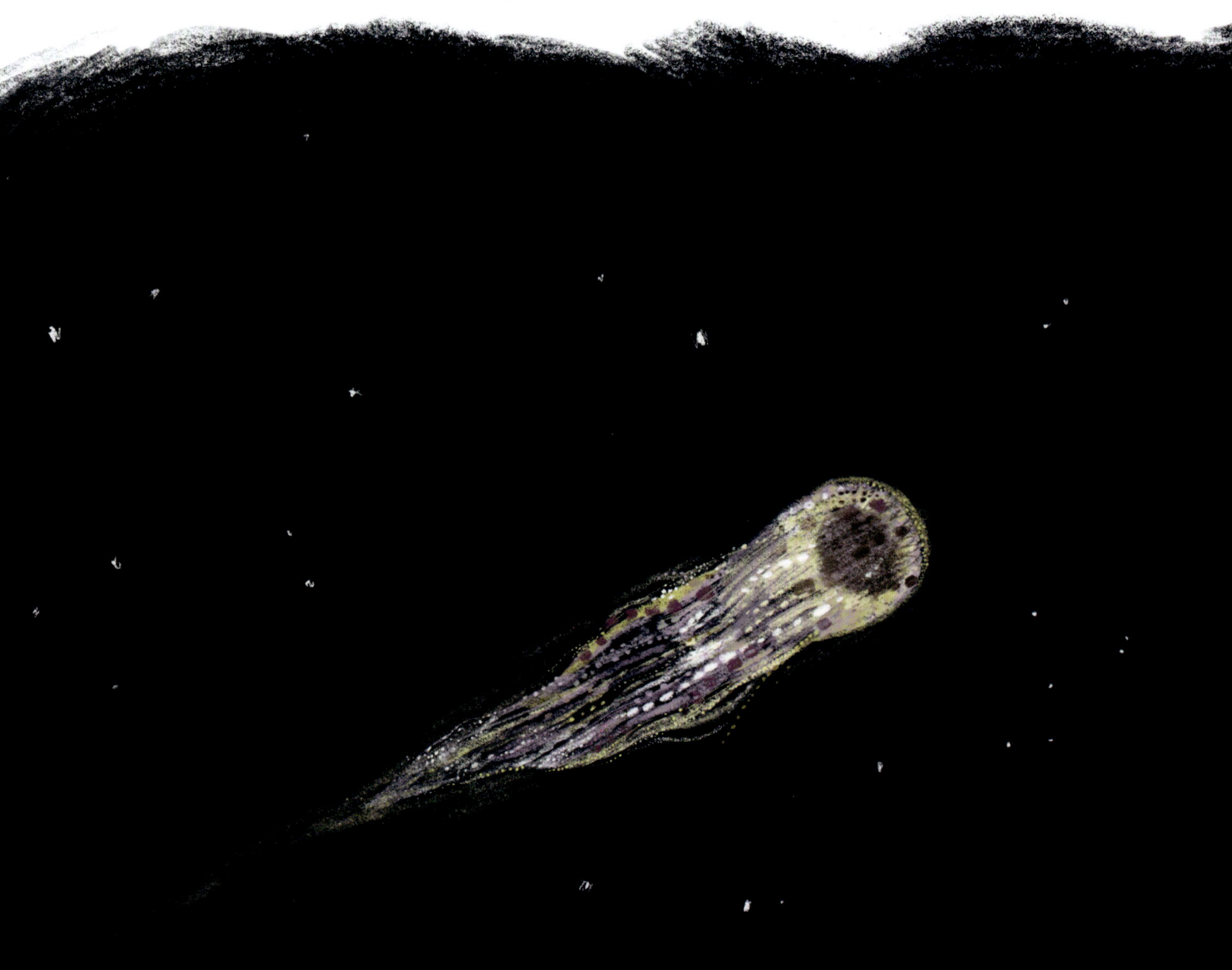

THE STORY OF EVERYTHING

The universe is born.	The sun is born.	Earth is born. Its surface cools.	Continents form.
13.8 billion years ago	4.6 billion years ago	Hadean Eon–4.6 to 4 billion years ago	Archean Eon–4 to 2.5 billion years ago
Scientists believe the universe began as a single point that grew bigger and bigger. The universe's birth is called "The Big Bang."	The sun is a star. It was created when a cloud of gas and dust collapsed into a swirling disk.	Planets formed from clumps of matter colliding in the sun's orbit.	Continents are large pieces of land that cover parts of Earth.

Dinosaurs and mammals roam on foot.	Bees carry pollen from blossom to blossom.	A giant asteroid hurtles toward Earth.	Soot fills the air. Dinosaurs disappear. Tsunamis and wildfires rage.
Mesozoic Era, Triassic Period–250 to 200 million years ago	Mesozoic Era, Cretaceous Period–145 to 66 million years ago	End of the Mesozoic Era–66 million years ago	Start of the Cenozoic Era–66 million years ago
The first dinosaurs and the first mammals appeared during the same period on Earth.	Bees and other pollinators allowed many types of flowers to evolve.	Scientists estimate that the asteroid was more than six miles wide.	The asteroid triggered a tsunami, wildfires, and changes to the gases around Earth. These events led to the extinction of many life-forms, including non-avian dinosaurs.

Sulfur steams. Bacteria grow.	Fish swim the seas.	Amphibians crawl and hop to land.	Wind scatters fern spores far and wide.
Archean Eon–4 to 2.5 billion years ago	Paleozoic Era, Ordovician Period–485 to 445 million years ago	Paleozoic Era, Devonian Period–420 to 360 million years ago	Paleozoic Era, Carboniferous Period–360 to 300 million years ago
Earth's earliest life-forms were bacteria.	Unlike the creatures that came before them, fish have backbones.	Amphibians can live in water or on land. Modern amphibians include frogs, toads, and salamanders.	A wide variety of ferns evolved during this time.

Life renews.	Primates swing from branch to branch.	Humans build, create, and play.	You are born.
Cenozoic Era–66 million years ago	Cenozoic Era, Paleogene Period–65 million years ago	Cenozoic Era, Quaternary Period–2.5 million years ago to present	Present day
Birds and small mammals were some of the animals that survived this mass extinction.	The earliest primates probably appeared about 65 million years ago.	Humans, also called *Homo sapiens*, are a type of primate.	You are one of more than 8 billion humans on Earth.

BIBLIOGRAPHY

Black, Riley. "What Happened the Day a Giant, Dinosaur-Killing Asteroid Hit the Earth." *Smithsonian Magazine*. 9 Sept. 2019, https://www.smithsonianmag.com/science-nature/dinosaur-killing-asteroid-impact-chicxu lub-crater-timeline-destruction-180973075/. Accessed 12 April 2020.

Boudreau, Diane, et al. "Continent." *National Geographic*. 20 Sept. 2011, https://www.nationalgeographic.org/encyclopedia/Continent/. Accessed 2 June 2021.

"Geologic Time Scale." National Parks Service, U.S. Department of the Interior. 26 Oct. 2018, www.nps.gov/subjects/geology/time-scale.htm. Accessed 12 April 2020.

Goulson, Dave. "The Beguiling History of Bees [Excerpt]." *Scientific American*. 25 April 2014, https://www.scientificamerican.com/article/the-beguiling-history-of-bees-excerpt/. Accessed 23 March 2020.

Holland, Steven M. "Ordovician Period." *Encyclopaedia Britannica*. Encyclopaedia Britannica, Inc. 17 May 2018, https://www.britannica.com/science/Ordovician-Period. Accessed 15 March 2020.

International Commission on Stratigraphy. "International Chronostratigraphic Chart." 2021, https://stratigraphy.org/ICSchart/ChronostratChart2021-05.pdf. Accessed 2 June 2021.

Lumen Learning. *Boundless Biology*. OER textbook. "Early Plant Life." https://courses.lumenlearning.com/boundless-biology/chapter/early-plant-life/. Accessed 18 June 2019.

Lumen Learning. *Boundless Biology*. OER textbook. "Seedless Vascular Plants." https://courses.lumenlearning.com/boundless-biology/chapter/seedless-vascular-plants/. Accessed 18 June 2019.

NASA. "Earth: In Depth." NASA Science. 19 Dec. 2019, https://solarsystem.nasa.gov/planets/earth/in-depth/#otp_formation/. Accessed 2 June 2021.

NASA. "Our Solar System: In Depth." NASA Science. 19 Dec. 2019, https://solarsystem.nasa.gov/solar-system/our-solar-system/in-depth/. Accessed 2 June 2021.

NASA. "What is the Big Bang?" NASA Science - Space Place. 27 June 2019, https://spaceplace.nasa.gov/big-bang/en/. Accessed 15 Sept. 2019.

Pennisi, Elizabeth. "How life blossomed after the dinosaurs died." *Science*. 24 Oct. 2019, https://www.sciencemag.org/news/2019/10/how-life-blossomed-after-dinosaurs-died. Accessed 15 July 2021.

Pennisi, Elizabeth. "Land Plants Arose Earlier than Thought—and May Have Had a Bigger Impact on the Evolution of Animals." *Science*. 19 Feb. 2018, www.sciencemag.org/news/2018/02/land-plants-arose-earlier-thought-and-may-have-had-bigger-impact-evolution-animals.

Rafferty, John P. "Hadean Eon." *Encyclopaedia Britannica*. Encyclopaedia Britannica, Inc. 21 May 2020, https://www.britannica.com/science/Hadean-Eon. Accessed 2 June 2021.

Rogers, Kara, and Robert J. Kadner. "Bacteria." *Encyclopaedia Britannica*. Encyclopaedia Britannica, Inc. 4 Dec. 2020, https://www.britannica.com/science/bacteria. Accessed 2 June 2021.

Singer, Emily. "How Dinosaurs Shrank and Became Birds." *Quanta Magazine*, Simons Foundation. 2 June 2015, https://www.quantamagazine.org/how-birds-evolved-from-dinosaurs-20150602. Accessed 19 Jan. 2020.

St. Fleur, Nicholas. "Where Did Fish First Evolve? The Answer May Be Shallow." *New York Times*. 25 October 2018, https://www.nytimes.com/2018/10/25/science/fish-evolution-shallow-coasts.html. Accessed 2 June 2021.

United States Census Bureau. "U.S. and World Population Clock." https://www.census.gov/popclock/. Accessed 16 July 2021.

Walker, Warren F., et al. "Fern." *Encyclopaedia Britannica*. Encyclopaedia Britannica, Inc. 14 February 2019, https://www.britannica.com/plant/fern. Accessed 28 Dec. 2019.

Wayman, Erin. "Five Early Primates You Should Know." *Smithsonian Magazine*, Smithsonian Institution. 31 Oct. 2012, https://www.smithsonianmag.com/science-nature/five-early-primates-you-should-know-102122862/. Accessed 12 Jan. 2020.

Weitzman, Stanley H., and Lynne R. Parenti. "Fish." *Encyclopaedia Britannica*. Encyclopaedia Britannica, Inc. 4 May 2021, https://www.britannica.com/animal/fish. Accessed 2 June 2021.

Windley, Brian Frederick. "Archean Eon." *Encyclopaedia Britannica*. Encyclopaedia Britannica, Inc. 11 April 2018, https://www.britannica.com/science/Archean-Eon. Accessed 15 Sept. 2019.

Zirin, Harold, and Kenneth Lang. "Sun." *Encyclopaedia Britannica*. Encyclopaedia Britannica, Inc. 5 February 2020, https://www.britannica.com/place/Sun. Accessed 22 March 2020.

Zug, George R., and William E. Duellman. "Amphibian." *Encyclopaedia Britannica*. Encyclopaedia Britannica, Inc. 4 March 2020, https://www.britannica.com/animal/amphibian. Accessed 16 March 2020.

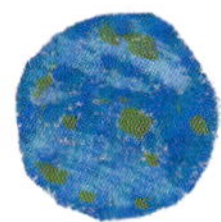

For my dad, El Pirata. Thanks for all the adventures.—K.N.

For AMMR—K.C.

The publisher would like to thank Mark Popinchalk, PhD, for the expert review of this book.

Printed and bound in January 2026 at C&C Offset, Shenzhen, China.
The artwork was created with Procreate and Apple Pencil.
www.holidayhouse.com
First Edition
1 3 5 7 9 10 8 6 4 2

Library of Congress Cataloging-in-Publication Data is available.

ISBN: 978-0-8234-5846-2 (hardcover)

EU Authorized Representative: HackettFlynn Ltd, 36 Cloch Choirneal, Balrothery,
Co. Dublin, K32 C942, Ireland. EU@walkerpublishinggroup.com